MARCUS
GARVEY

BLACK NATIONALIST CRUSADER AND ENTREPRENEUR

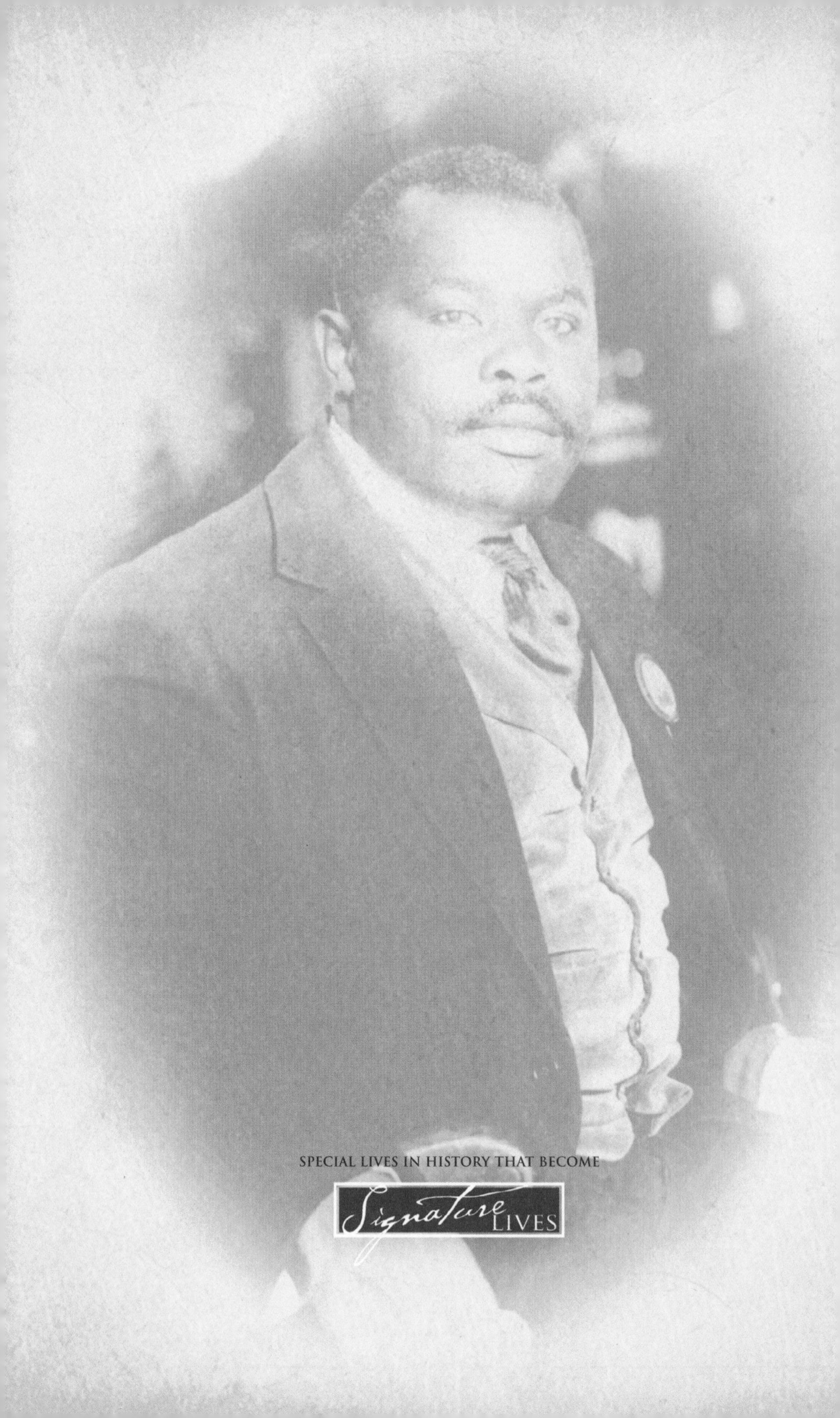

SPECIAL LIVES IN HISTORY THAT BECOME

Signature LIVES

MARCUS

GARVEY

BLACK NATIONALIST CRUSADER AND ENTREPRENEUR

by Brenda Haugen

Content Adviser: Keith Mayes, Ph.D., Assistant Professor,
Department of African American and African Studies,
University of Minnesota

Reading Adviser: Rosemary G. Palmer, Ph.D.,
Department of Literacy, College of Education,
Boise State University

Compass Point Books ✦ Minneapolis, Minnesota

Compass Point Books
3109 West 50th Street, #115
Minneapolis, MN 55410

 This book was manufactured with paper containing at least
10 percent post-consumer waste.

Editor: Jennifer VanVoorst
Page Production: Ashlee Schultz
Photo Researcher: Svetlana Zhurkin
Cartographer: XNR Productions, Inc.
Library Consultant: Kathleen Baxter

Creative Director: Keith Griffin
Editorial Director: Nick Healy
Managing Editor: Catherine Neitge

Library of Congress Cataloging-in-Publication Data
Haugen, Brenda.
  Marcus Garvey : black nationalist crusader and entrepreneur / by
Brenda Haugen.
    p. cm. — (Signature lives)
  Includes bibliographical references and index.
  ISBN 978-0-7565-3626-8 (library binding)
  1. Garvey, Marcus, 1887–1940—Juvenile literature. 2. African
Americans—Biography—Juvenile literature. 3. Jamaican Americans—
Biography—Juvenile literature. 4. Universal Negro Improvement
Association—Juvenile literature. 5. Black nationalism—Juvenile literature.
I. Title. II. Series.
  E185.97.G3H39 2008
  305.8'96073—dc22
  [B]   2007035561

Visit Compass Point Books on the Internet at *www.compasspointbooks.com*
or e-mail your request to *custserv@compasspointbooks.com*

MODERN WORLD

From 1900 to the present day, the world and its people have undergone major changes. Worldwide wars and other major conflicts have cost millions of lives and thrown humanity into turmoil. Fascism and communism divided some countries, and democracy brought others together. Political openness and the acceptance of new ideas gave hope to many. And as rapid technological advancements brought the world's citizens closer together, they illuminated the need for global understanding and cooperation.

Table of Contents

1 The UNIA Conference

Chapter

❦

According to Marcus Garvey, August 1, 1920, was "a red letter day for the Negro peoples of the world." On that day, the first International Convention of the Negro Peoples of the World opened in New York City. About 25,000 delegates from 25 countries attended the opening session at Madison Square Garden. They traveled from African countries such as Nigeria, Sierra Leone, Liberia, and South Africa. They came from West Indian countries such as Cuba, Haiti, Trinidad, Barbados, and Jamaica. There were also delegates from the United States, Canada, England, and France.

The convention was sponsored by the Universal Negro Improvement Association (UNIA). The UNIA preached racial pride and called for blacks to be self-

Marcus Garvey signed a portrait of himself in his uniform as the provisional president of Africa.

sufficient. It was also dedicated to setting up schools for blacks, improving the conditions of blacks worldwide, and founding a new, independent black nation in Africa.

The group's Black Star Line Band and the Liberty Hall Choir opened the meeting with familiar black hymns, and an impressive parade followed as the convention-goers moved from Liberty Hall to Madison Square Garden. Marcus Garvey, the leader of the UNIA, looked regal in a military-style uniform with a plumed hat. One spectator said, "When Garvey rode by … I got an emotional lift which swept me up above the poverty and prejudice by which my life was limited." The entire crowd was swept with a feeling of hopefulness and pride by the proceedings.

When Garvey stepped forward to deliver the opening address, he received a five-minute standing ovation. In his speech, he talked about his mission to overturn white rule in Africa and reclaim the continent for the world's black population. "It is a political calling for me to redeem Africa," he told the crowd.

Garvey's speech energized his supporters, but it frightened others. He said, "We are coming, four hundred million strong, and we mean to retake every square inch of the twelve million square miles of African territory belonging to us by right divine."

During the convention, which lasted the entire

month, the UNIA adopted a Declaration of the Rights of the Negro Peoples of the World. The declaration detailed the group's grievances and demanded that they be addressed. Among the things the group asked for were the teaching of black history in classrooms and an end to discrimination.

Marcus Garvey was driven through the streets of Harlem in New York City during the 1920 UNIA convention.

The group chose a flag to represent its "nation" with the colors of red, black, and green. Each color was chosen to symbolize one element of the black struggle. Red represented blood that had been shed for freedom, black stood for the black skin of the people, and green symbolized the lush landscape of the African homeland.

Garvey was elected the "provisional president of Africa," a government he considered to be in exile. Because there was and still is no country called Africa, the title of president of Africa was only symbolic and referred to the eventual unity of black Africa.

The monthlong convention brought Marcus Garvey and his organization worldwide attention. Though it energized black people, many white

Members of the Black Cross Nurses, a group within the UNIA, marched through the streets of Harlem during the UNIA convention.

leaders were suspicious of Garvey and the UNIA. The UNIA was calling for the blacks of the world to take back Africa. At the time, most of Africa was governed by European nations that seemed to care more for the continent's many natural resources than for the people who lived there. Only Liberia and Ethiopia remained under black control. Garvey dreamed of a day when all of Africa was governed by blacks.

Garvey's call for "Africa for Africans" arose not from a hatred of other races but from a deep love for his own race. Garvey saw increasing educational opportunities for blacks. He believed that, in time, better-educated blacks would compete with whites for powerful jobs. He feared that this competition would, in 50 to 100 years, lead to clashes between the races that would end disastrously for blacks. He worried that the black race would be destroyed. By reclaiming Africa as the black homeland, Garvey hoped, such a devastating result for his people could be avoided. But he believed that the lives of black people around the world would not be improved until they took control of their own destinies. He said:

> *We are determined to solve our own problem, by redeeming our Motherland Africa from the hands of alien exploiters and found there a Government, a nation of our own, strong enough to lend protection*

Marcus Garvey delivered the opening address at the 1920 UNIA convention.

to the members of our race scattered all over the world, and to compel the respect of the nations and races of the earth.

At the same time, however, Garvey believed that all races needed one another. He said in a November 1922 speech:

> *We are not preaching a propaganda of hate against anybody. We love the white man; we love all humanity, because we feel that we cannot live without the other. The white man is as necessary to the existence of the Negro as the Negro is necessary to his existence. There is a common relationship that we cannot escape.*

Garvey took his message around the world. At the height of its popularity, the UNIA had branches in every area of the world where a significant black population was found. They were established in North America, Australia, and Europe. In the United States, 38 states had UNIA members. By 1920, Garvey claimed the organization's membership worldwide to be about 2 million.

Many people saw Marcus Garvey as a threat. Some governments believed he inspired blacks to challenge their authority by challenging the racism that allowed them to rule. Some blacks believed Garvey was wrong for preaching separation of races while they were trying to win equality. But Garvey stayed true to his goal, though it nearly cost him his freedom and his life. 🐎

2 GROWING UP IN JAMAICA

Chapter

❦

Marcus Mosiah Garvey was born August 17, 1887, in St. Ann's Bay, Jamaica. He was the youngest of 11 children born to Marcus and Sarah Garvey. Only Marcus and his sister Indiana lived to adulthood. Marcus' father, for whom he was named, worked as a master mason, creating beautiful work from brick and stone. He was a smart man who read a great deal and even served as a local lawyer.

Because Marcus' father would rather read than work, the Garvey family often relied on his mother, who earned money by farming a plot of land with her brother. They grew citrus and allspice trees. She also sold baked goods to raise money for her family.

At that time, Jamaica was a British colony. Both parents were descendants of African slaves who had

The Kingston, Jamaica, harbor in 1905

Jamaica is part of the West Indies, a chain of islands that divides the Caribbean Sea from the Atlantic Ocean. Jamaica was a British colony for more than 300 years. The British invaded Jamaica in 1655 and took formal possession of the island nation 15 years later. However, the British faced challenges from the Maroons, a group of African slaves who had escaped to the hills when the British invaded Jamaica. After years of fighting, the British finally signed a peace treaty with the Maroons in 1738. Included in the treaty was the Maroons' right to tax-free land. In 1962, Jamaica became an independent nation. More than nine of every 10 Jamaican citizens have black African or mixed black African and European ancestry.

been brought to the West Indies by the British to work on the sugarcane plantations. Garvey later recalled:

My father was a man of brilliant intellect and dashing courage. He was unafraid of consequences. He took human chances in the course of his life as most bold men do, and he failed at the close of his career. He once had a fortune; he died poor. My poor mother was a sober and conscientious Christian, too soft and good for the time in which she lived. She was the direct opposite of my father. He was severe, firm, determined, bold and strong, refusing to yield even to superior forces if he believed he was right. My mother, on the other hand, was always willing to return a smile for a blow, and ever ready to bestow charity upon her enemy.

Life likely wouldn't have been as difficult for the Garveys if not for the stubbornness of Marcus' father. A descendant of the Maroons, escaped slaves who fought British colonial rule, he had inherited land in Jamaica. However, he eventually lost almost all of this land in court battles with neighbors and over debts he refused to pay.

Maroons in Jamaica in the early 20th century

Young Marcus attended the grammar school in St. Ann's Bay and the Church of England High School. He also was tutored by the Reverend W.H. Sloely and the Reverend P.A. Conahan. Throughout his life, Marcus understood the importance of education, and he loved to read, just like his father. He also enjoyed riding his bicycle around the village and swimming in the bay.

Children attending school in Jamaica in 1904

As a young boy, Marcus went to school and played with both black children and white children. He recalled:

> To me, at home in my early days, there was no difference between white and black. One of my father's properties, the place where I lived most of the time, was adjoining that of a white man. He had three girls and two boys ... another white man, whose church my parents attended, also had property adjoining ours. He had three girls and one boy. All of us were playmates. We romped and were happy children, playmates together. The little white girl whom I liked most knew no better than I did myself. We were two innocent fools who never dreamed of a race feeling and problem.

Seeming to foreshadow the life her son would lead, Garvey's mother, Sarah, had wanted to give her son the middle name Moses, because she hoped he would be like Moses in the Bible and lead his people to freedom. His father, however, insisted upon the less prominent biblical middle name of Mosiah. As a child, he went by the nickname "Moses" or "Mose," as well as "Ugly Mug."

However, everything changed when Marcus was 14 years old. The little white girl's parents decided the time had come to end the friendship between the two children. Garvey said:

> They sent her and another sister to Edinburgh, Scotland, and told her that she was never to write or try to get in

In Jamaica in the late 1800s, there was a direct relationship between skin color and economic and social status. White people held the most wealth and power, followed by mulattoes, people with mixed European and African ancestry. People of unmixed African ancestry, like the Garveys, generally lived in poverty and faced discrimination. As an adult, Marcus Garvey reacted against this environment, encouraging his followers to take pride in their African heritage and expressing distrust of all but the darkest-skinned black people.

touch with me. ... It was then that I found for the first time that there was some difference in humanity, and that there were different races, each having its own separate and distinct social life. I did not care about the separation after I was told about it because I never thought all during our childhood association that the girl and the rest of the children of her race were better than I was; in fact, they used to look up to me. So I simply had no regrets.

Marcus had hoped to continue his education at a secondary school in Kingston, the capital of Jamaica. But his family was struggling financially, and he felt a responsibility to help. At 14 years of age, he quit school to work full time for his godfather, Alfred Burrowes. As an apprentice at Burrowes' print shop in St. Ann's Bay, he learned the printer's trade by day, and in the evening, he educated himself by reading books from his godfather's library.

Because St. Ann's Bay was a small town, Burrowes'

print shop was not very busy. When he had learned all he could, Marcus decided it was time to strike out for the big city and better opportunities. ☙

Students at Alabama's Tuskegee Institute learned the printing trade.

3 ON HIS OWN

ෙගංචං

*I*n 1906, 18-year-old Marcus Garvey left home for Kingston, where he found work as a printer at his uncle's print shop, the P.A. Benjamin Manufacturing Company. He excelled at his job, and two years later, he was rewarded for his efforts by being promoted to master printer and foreman. At 20, he was the youngest foreman printer in the city.

Garvey also became active in the printers union. When members of the group decided to strike for better wages, they chose Garvey as their leader. In the end, the strike failed when foreign workers were brought in to replace those on strike. Because of his role in the strike, no private printer would hire Garvey. However, he was able to find a job with the government printing office.

A 19th-century illustration of Jamaicans taking their produce to market

Garvey thrived in Kingston. He enjoyed the hustle and bustle of the large city. He also loved the city's political scene. Right on the street, people engaged in lively debates about the issues of the day. Garvey soon took his turn expressing his opinions. At first, people made fun of him because he didn't express himself well. Nothing in his background had prepared him for public speaking. But Garvey didn't give up.

Kingston, Jamaica, had a bustling street scene that energized Marcus Garvey.

He decided the best way to improve as a speaker was to learn from the examples of others. Realizing that some of the most powerful speakers could

be found in the pulpit, Garvey sought out the best preachers in the city and went to their churches every week. He listened to their phrasing and watched their gestures. At home, Garvey practiced what he learned in front of a mirror. He also began carrying a pocket dictionary and looking up words he didn't understand. His hard work quickly paid off. He continued to share his thoughts on the city's street corners, but more and more people paused to listen to what he had to say—and they no longer made fun of his style.

Garvey's experience leading the printers' strike had helped him understand the need for organized action to improve the lot of the black worker. When he was 21 years old, Garvey began publishing his own newspaper, *Garvey's Watchman*. Though the newspaper went out of business after only three issues were published, Garvey would edit and publish newspapers for much of his life.

Garvey joined the National Club, a group that discussed the problems Jamaica had with its colonial rulers. He also edited

As a printer, Marcus Garvey learned that the written word could be very powerful. It was natural for him to turn to the written word when he decided he wanted to make a difference in the lives of black people living in Jamaica. The first issue of Garvey's Watchman was published in 1909. Garvey hoped the small newspaper would bring attention to the plight of Jamaica's black workers and lead to improved working conditions and better wages.

that organization's weekly paper, *Our Own*. But Garvey wanted to do more. He wanted to build an organization that would wield real power to make life better for blacks in Jamaica—better jobs, better wages, and more political control.

Garvey knew that in order to build the kind of organization he wanted, he would need money, and he felt that his prospects were brighter outside his home country. In 1910, he decided to venture to Costa Rica. He thought he might be able to make enough money there to build his organization back home. He expected to work a short time before returning to Jamaica to continue the struggle for black rights in his homeland. However, it would not be that easy.

In Costa Rica, Garvey worked at a United Fruit Company plantation, a job his uncle found for him. His responsibility was to keep track of the number of hours the employees worked. Garvey witnessed the hard work and dangers faced by other blacks who worked for the company. The swamps where the bananas grew were filled with dangerous animals. And those weren't the only

The United Fruit Company was often criticized by journalists and politicians, both in the United States and abroad, for exploiting workers and doing little to help improve conditions in the countries where its plantations were located. Though it had a monopoly in some regions, in others it faced tough competition from other companies. United Fruit was often accused of bribing government officials to gain preferential treatment over its competitors.

Workers cut bananas from trees in Costa Rica.

dangers. Thieves often stole the workers' money—and sometimes took their lives, too.

Angry about the terrible working conditions and dangers workers faced, Garvey moved to Puerto Limón, Costa Rica, where he tried to get officials at the British consulate to address these problems. Although they worked in Costa Rica, an independent nation, many of the workers were residents of islands controlled by Great Britain. Garvey knew it was the British consulate's duty to protect these citizens. But no one at the consulate would listen to him.

Garvey decided to appeal directly to the people of Costa Rica. In an effort to organize local blacks and force change, Garvey created the daily newspaper *La Nacionale*. But again Garvey met with disappointment. Afraid to stir up trouble and lose what little they had, Costa Ricans ignored Garvey's calls to organize.

Black field-workers drilled holes for blasting during construction of the Panama Canal.

Garvey moved on to Panama, where he found another grim situation for those of his race. Blacks who were helping build the Panama Canal faced

malaria and other dangerous diseases. They also did the hardest work, and they were paid less than white workers and lived in poorer housing. In short, black workers were treated like second-class citizens. Garvey found the same conditions in Nicaragua, Venezuela, Columbia, and other Central American and South American countries where he traveled. He became convinced that white rulers valued the lives of white citizens more than those of black citizens.

After suffering a bout of malaria himself, Garvey returned to Jamaica in 1912, but he didn't stay long. Soon after his return, he traveled to England. He believed he might have a better chance of making a difference for black citizens if he went directly to where British policy was made.

Garvey went to London and found work at the docks. In his new job, he met black sailors from the United States, Africa, and other parts of the world. In talking with them, Garvey realized that the problems blacks faced in Jamaica and the rest of the Caribbean were the same problems blacks faced in all parts of

Completed in 1914, the Panama Canal was designed to create a link between the Atlantic and Pacific oceans through the Isthmus of Panama. Stretching for about 51 miles (82 kilometers), the canal cost $375 million and took a decade to construct. It was built by the United States under a 1903 treaty with Panama and took the work of thousands of laborers toiling in hot, moist, and dangerous conditions.

the world. He later recalled his journey of discovery:

I started to take an interest in the politics of my country, and then I saw the injustice done to my race because it was black. ... I went traveling to South and Central America and parts of the West Indies to find out if it was so elsewhere, and I found the same situation. I set sail for Europe to find out if it was different there, and again I found the same stumbling block—"You are black."

Garvey spent much of his life in the area known as the West Indies.

Map shows modern boundaries.

UNITED STATES

Atlantic Ocean

Gulf of Mexico

BAHAMAS

Havana

Sagua La Grande

CUBA

West Indies

HAITI

MEXICO

St. Ann's Bay

JAMAICA   Kingston

BELIZE

DOMINICAN REPUBLIC

GUATEMALA   HONDURAS

Caribbean Sea

EL SALVADOR   NICARAGUA

0   300 miles
0   300 kilometers

Puerto Limón

Bocas del Toro

Colón

NORTH AMERICA

SOUTH AMERICA

COSTA RICA   PANAMA

VENEZUELA

COLOMBIA

Pacific Ocean

While working at the docks, Garvey satisfied his desire for learning by attending London's Birkbeck College. Birkbeck was a school for people who worked full time and had neither the time nor the money to attend a regular university. He spent 18 months studying law, history, and philosophy. He also spent hours reading about the history and culture of Africa. He learned about the great black leaders and the civilizations that had thrived in Africa before Europeans first came to the continent in the 1400s. Schools didn't teach about these great civilizations and their contributions to art, music, religion, and government. It was a great awakening for Garvey.

After traveling around Western Europe, Garvey again came back to Jamaica in the summer of 1914. However, he was a different person from when he had left. He felt he had a mission on a bigger scale. And it was a book that had helped lead him to that conclusion.

The Songhay Empire was a black kingdom in West Africa that reached its peak during the 1400s and 1500s. Songhay's great leaders included King Sunni Ali, who in 1464 conquered the fabled city of Timbuktu, which today is in the country of Mali. King Askia the Great expanded the kingdom after coming to power in 1493. He encouraged the spread of Islam and expanded trade. The empire's power declined after its defeat by a Moroccan army at the Battle of Tondibi in 1591.

BIG MASS MEETING

A CALL TO THE
COLORED CITIZENS

OF

ATLANTA, GEORGIA

To Hear the Great West Indian Negro Leader

HON. MARCUS GARVEY

President of the Universal Negro Improvement Association
of Jamaica, West Indies.

Big Bethel A. M. E. Church

Corner Auburn Avenue and Butler Street

SUNDAY AFTERNOON, AT 3 O'CLOCK
MARCH 25, 1917

He brings a message of inspiration to the
12,000,000 of our people in this country.

SUBJECT:

"The Negroes of the West Indies, afte
78 years of Emancipation." With
general talk on the world position o
the race.

An orator of exceptional force, Professor Garvey has spoke
to packed audiences in England, New York, Boston, Washingtor
Philadelphia, Chicago, Milwaukee, St. Louis, Detroit, Clevelanc
Cincinatti, Indianapolis, Louisville, Nashville and other cities. H
has travelled to the principal countries of Europe, and was th
first Negro to speak to the Veterans' Club of London, Englanc

This is the only chance to hear a great man who has take
his message before the world. **COME OUT EARLY T**
SECURE SEATS. It is worth travelling 1,000 miles to hear.

All Invited. Rev. R. H. Singleton, D.D., Pasto

4 FOUNDING THE UNIA

ᴄᵌⲭᵌᴐ

As he became an adult, Marcus Garvey discovered there was a real split between the white and black races. White boys he had befriended as a child would no longer have anything to do with him as they now forged their own careers. In his own country and during his travels abroad, Garvey discovered that blacks found it difficult or impossible to advance in their jobs or to take part in government. He recalled:

> At maturity the black and white boys separated, and took different courses in life. My schoolmates as young men did not know or remember me any more. Then I realized that I had to make a fight for a place in the world, that it was not so easy to pass on to office and position.

A 1917 handbill invited African-Americans to a mass meeting led by UNIA leader Marcus Garvey in Atlanta, Georgia.

Then Garvey read *Up from Slavery* by American author and educator Booker T. Washington, and it changed his life. In the book, Washington said blacks needed to improve themselves through hard work and education before they would be accepted as equals in society by whites. Garvey recalled:

> I read Up from Slavery ... *and then my doom—if I may so call it—of being a race leader dawned upon me. I asked: "Where is the black man's government? ... Where is his President, his country, and ... his men of big affairs?" I could not find them, and then I declared, "I will help to make them."*

After reading the book, Garvey became consumed with the idea of "uniting all the Negro peoples of the world into one great body to establish a country and Government absolutely their own." He took the first step when he arrived back in Kingston in 1914. On August 1, he formed the Universal Negro Improvement Association. The UNIA slogan, "One God! One Aim!

One Destiny!" expressed the "Universal Confraternity [brotherhood] among the race" that was a key part of the group's mission. The UNIA also supported the founding of an independent black nation in Africa. Though two African nations were run by black governments, most of the continent was controlled by European powers. Garvey was among those who believed that Africa was the black race's homeland and needed to be governed by blacks.

At the turn of the 20th century, the continent of Africa was largely governed by European powers. Only Liberia and Ethiopia were both independent and black-run.

Africa, 1920
- Belgian
- British
- Formerly German
- French
- Italian
- Portuguese
- Spanish
- South African
- Independent

The organization grew slowly. It boasted only about 100 members after its first year. But Garvey was not discouraged. He made plans to travel to the United States to raise money for the UNIA. He also planned to meet Booker T. Washington. He and Washington had been exchanging letters, and Garvey was excited about meeting the man in person. However, it was not to be. Washington died on November 14, 1915, just months before Garvey was to leave for the United States. Garvey was saddened by the loss of Washington, but he decided to continue with his trip to the United States anyway.

Booker T.
Washington
(1856–1915)

After arriving in the United States in March 1916, Garvey found a place to live in Harlem, a neighborhood in New York City, and got a job as a printer. Garvey saved all the money he could. He planned to tour the United States to raise money for the UNIA.

Garvey didn't like what he saw in the United States. He believed America's black leaders had no real plan to make life better for their race. Garvey saw many of them as people who used their positions of leadership to do nothing more than better their own lives.

Garvey spent almost every spare moment promoting the UNIA. In a short time, he had raised enough money to embark on a speaking tour that took him to 38 states and lasted about a year.

Garvey put the speaking skills he had developed on the streets of Kingston to good use. He proved to be a skilled orator. He memorized the outlines of his most important speeches, but most of the time he just spoke freely—not confined by a set of notes. He also didn't like to be confined by others' ideas. He knew what he believed and boldly said so. Throughout his life, Garvey didn't look to others for advice or their opinions, and he didn't shy away from controversy.

Garvey encouraged his listeners to take pride in their African heritage. He also talked about conditions in Jamaica and listened to others describe their lives in the United States. More and more people flocked to hear Garvey's message of black pride. In time, thousands of people would gather to hear Garvey speak. He reached millions of others through newspapers.

When he returned to New York in May 1917, a group of 13 gathered in a dingy Harlem basement to create the New York branch of the UNIA. Not only

Harlem in the early 1900s was a bustling center for black culture. The area gave rise to a flourishing of the arts and intellectual thought that became known as the Harlem Renaissance. Many famous black poets, artists, and thinkers lived and worked in Harlem during that time, including Langston Hughes, Zora Neale Hurston, and Charles Gilpin.

did Garvey live in Harlem, but the neighborhood also served as the headquarters of his organization and the base for his many publications. Chief among them was his weekly newspaper, *The Negro World*, which had readers around the world.

The first issue of *The Negro World*, the official newspaper of the UNIA, was published on August 17, 1918, Garvey's 31st birthday. It shared the stories of black heroes and spread Garvey's message of black pride. Garvey also used *The Negro World* to express his opinions, including his belief that blacks would only be respected when they gained economic power.

Some governments in other countries saw the newspaper as a threat, and several ordered it banned or confiscated. Among them were the governments of British Honduras (present-day Belize) and British Guiana, which seized copies of the newspaper sent there.

Garvey also shared his message through speeches he gave at Liberty Hall, an auditorium the UNIA purchased in Harlem. There he talked about

The Harlem neighborhood in New York City was the center of a cultural flourishing among African-Americans in the early 20th century.

the beauty of black culture and the great history of the race. He worked to instill in others the pride he felt while reading about the history of the African continent before white colonial rule. He also told his audiences that blacks would only gain the respect of the world by becoming economically strong. And he was going to show them how to accomplish that goal. ☙

5 GOING INTO BUSINESS

❦

In 1919, Marcus Garvey made a bold move. In an effort to show his followers that blacks could gain economic independence, he established a shipping company called the Black Star Line. This company would promote commerce among black people worldwide by transporting manufactured goods and raw materials among black-run businesses in Africa, the Caribbean, and the Americas.

African-American, West Indian, and African merchants welcomed the opportunity to work with the Black Star Line. They hoped this new shipping line would deal more fairly with them than some of the white companies did. Garvey believed the Black Star Line would find plenty of business just dealing

Marcus Garvey established the Black Star Line to encourage commerce among people of African ancestry throughout the world.

with black merchants and companies.

Black Star Line ships would also carry passengers. Unlike other shipping lines, the Black Star Line would not treat black passengers like second-class citizens. Those working on the ships wouldn't face discrimination either. On other shipping lines, blacks were often the last hired and the first fired. That wouldn't be the case on the Black Star Line.

Through advertisements in *The Negro World* and other publications, Garvey offered blacks the chance to buy stock in the company at $5 per share. The proposition was very exciting. This would be a major shipping line that would be owned and operated entirely by blacks.

Garvey's followers didn't let him down. They bought more than $600,000 worth of stock in the Black Star Line's first year. Many who invested couldn't really afford to spend $5 on a share of stock, but they were willing to make great personal sacrifices to be a part of this historic shipping line and help it become a success.

The Black Star Line incorporated, or officially became a business, on June 27, 1919. In less than three months, the company had enough money, mostly from stock sales, to buy its first ship. On September 17, 1919, the company signed a contract to buy the *Yarmouth* at $165,000. Though the ship was in poor condition and likely wasn't worth its

LET'S PUT IT OVER

The Indispensable Weekly
The Voice of the Awakened Negro

THE
Negro World

Reaching the Mass of Negroes
The Best Advertising Medium

A Newspaper Devoted Solely to the Interests of the Negro Race

XVII. No. 2   NEW YORK, SATURDAY, AUGUST 23, 1924   PRICE: FIVE CENTS IN GREATER NEW YORK, TEN CENTS ELSEWHERE IN THE U.S.A. TEN CENTS IN FOREIGN COUNTRIES

NEW NEGRO STEAMSHIP COMPANY SECURES FIRST SHIP FOR AFRICA

price tag, the shipping line was now very real.

Joshua Cockburn was hired to serve as the *Yarmouth*'s captain. Cockburn had experience sailing to African ports and was one of the few blacks of his day qualified to hold the post.

The front page of Garvey's newspaper, The Negro World, announced the acquisition of the Black Star Line's first steamship.

The *Yarmouth*'s first voyage was a short one. Garvey had problems securing insurance for the ship, along with other financial difficulties, but the *Yarmouth*'s owners agreed to let him sail the vessel from the 135th Street dock, near the UNIA Harlem office, to 23rd Street. Thousands gathered along the shore on October 31, 1919, to witness this short but historic trip.

A few weeks later, the *Yarmouth*—now unofficially named the *Frederick Douglass*—sailed on its first real voyage. Partially loaded with some passengers and a cargo of cement, the ship headed

The Black Star
Line's first ship was
named after Frederick
Douglass. Douglass
was born into slavery
in the United States
in 1818 but grew up
to become one of the
great leaders of his
race. A runaway slave,
Douglass risked his
freedom and life to start
an anti-slavery newspa-
per and send his story
across the country. He
also served as a leader
during the Civil War,
enlisting a group of
black men to fight for
the Union cause.

for Sagua La Grande, Cuba.

According to Captain Cockburn, people in Cuba greeted the ship with great excitement. After sailing on to Jamaica and Panama, the *Yarmouth* returned to the United States in January 1920, filled to capacity with passengers and cargo.

The next trip was not as successful. Just two days after its arrival back home, the ship was hired to take a load of whiskey to Cuba. Garvey had originally turned down the contract because the fee of about $7,000 wasn't enough to cover the cost of the journey. In addition, the *Yarmouth* needed repairs. However, according to Garvey, others in the company agreed to the contract while he was out of town. This was among the first acts of mismanagement that would plague the Black Star Line.

Not far into the journey, the *Yarmouth* was forced to return to shore for repairs. While still at sea, however, Cockburn ordered that 500 cases of whiskey and champagne be thrown overboard to lighten the damaged ship's load. Mysteriously, small boats were there to retrieve the cargo. It's unlikely

The S.S. Yarmouth was inspected by UNIA members.

that it was a lucky coincidence, but no plot to steal the cargo was ever uncovered.

After being repaired, the ship made a second attempt to get to Cuba with whiskey and passengers. On March 3, the *Yarmouth* arrived in Havana, Cuba, to great fanfare. The country's president honored the crew with a lavish banquet at his palace. He recognized the historic importance of a black shipping line's making a successful journey. The president and local businessmen promised the Black Star Line continued business.

But there was trouble to come. Black Star Line officials responsible for signing the contract hadn't found a consignee in Cuba—a person who would be responsible for the cargo once it arrived. With no one to take the whiskey, the ship had to sit in port and wait—and so did the 35 passengers who were planning to sail on with the ship to other locations. Additional delays followed, and the ship ended up staying in Cuba for 32 days. During that time, the Black Star Line kept losing money. While the *Yarmouth* sat idle, it couldn't make money hauling other cargo. In addition, the crew still had to be paid for its time, and the Black Star Line was responsible for taking care of the passengers who were stranded in Havana until the ship could set sail again.

When it finally got under way, the *Yarmouth* received rousing welcomes at each stop along its route. Hundreds of people welcomed the ship when it arrived in Jamaica. An even greater greeting awaited it in Colón, Panama.

"Literally thousands of Panamanians swarmed the docks with baskets of fruit, vegetables and gifts," said Hugh Mulzac, a black officer on the ship. "I

The Black Star Line office was located in the Harlem neighborhood of New York City.

was amazed that the *Yarmouth* had become such a symbol for colored people of every land."

He was even more amazed by the response in Bocas del Toro, Panama. Mulzac said:

Thousands of peasants came down from the hills on horses, donkeys, and in makeshift carts, and by a special train provided by the United Fruit Company, which, since it was going to lose its employees for the day anyway, declared a legal holiday. The crowd on the dock was so thick that when we threw our heavy lines ashore the peasants seized the hangars as they came out of the water and literally breasted us alongside the dock. In the tumult that followed dancing broke out on the deck, great piles of fruit and flowers mounted on the hatch covers, and U.N.I.A agents signed up hundreds of new members.

However, the ship faced more problems later in the journey. Seven hundred tons of coconuts picked up in Jamaica rotted before the vessel made it back to New York, and the Black Star Line had to pay the owners for the value of their ruined cargo.

In about two years of service, the *Yarmouth* never made money. In November 1921, it was sold for $1,625, a fraction of what Garvey had paid for it.

During its existence, the Black Star Line owned two more ships—the *Shadyside* and the *Kanawha*—but neither fared any better. The *Shadyside* cost $35,000 and was used for pleasure cruises along the Hudson River. It would last just one season before it sank following an ice storm. The *Kanawha*

The Shadyside *sank after only one season of service.*

was purchased for $65,000 and was expected to sail between New York and the West Indies as the *Yarmouth* did. However, the *Kanawha* was plagued with mechanical problems from the beginning. After a series of engine problems, the ship was abandoned at Antilla, Cuba.

The Black Star Line tried but failed to buy a fourth ship, the *Phyllis Wheatley*. It was meant to carry passengers from New York to Liberia, a country on the coast of Africa where Garvey hoped to set up a black settlement. He planned to use this settlement as a springboard for his efforts to take back Africa and return control of the continent to blacks.

Meanwhile, Garvey's influence continued to grow. By August 1921, the UNIA had 859 branches worldwide. No other black man in history had been able to unite so many people across the world in the cause of independence and defiance of colonialism and oppression.

The UNIA membership card of Mndindwa Marwanqana from South Africa

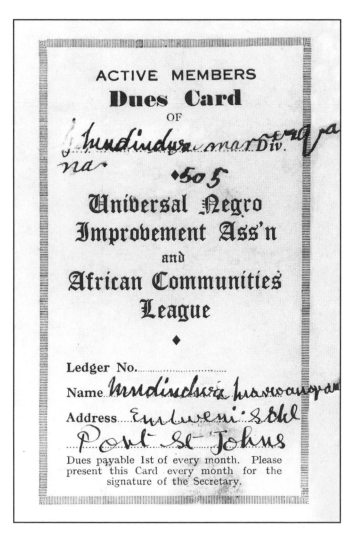

ACTIVE MEMBERS

Dues Card

OF

𝕌𝕟𝕚𝕧𝕖𝕣𝕤𝕒𝕝 𝕹𝕖𝕘𝕣𝕠
𝕁𝕞𝕡𝕣𝕠𝕧𝕖𝕞𝕖𝕟𝕥 𝕬𝕤𝕤'𝕟

and

𝕬𝕗𝕣𝕚𝕔𝕒𝕟 ℭ𝕠𝕞𝕞𝕦𝕟𝕚𝕥𝕚𝕖𝕤
𝕷𝕖𝕒𝕘𝕦𝕖

◆

Ledger No.

Name

Address

Dues payable 1st of every month. Please present this Card every month for the signature of the Secretary.

But while the UNIA was growing, the Black Star Line was suffering severe financial problems. During the summer of 1922, the shipping line went out of business after three years in operation. Yet Garvey refused to give up. In the next two years, he tried other business ventures, including another shipping company. His followers stood firmly behind him.

Garvey also launched the Negro Factories Corporation. The goal of the corporation was to build and operate factories in the United States, the West Indies, Africa, and Central America. Not only did the factories employ black workers, but blacks owned the businesses. For $1 per share, a black person could buy stock in the Negro Factories Corporation.

Though the corporation was never as grand as Garvey's vision, it did manage several businesses in Harlem. Among them were a doll factory, laundries, restaurants, a printing business, and a chain of grocery stores.

Even though the Black Star Line was a financial disaster and the Negro Factories Corporation was just a modest success, these ventures showed blacks that opportunities existed for them that they never before thought possible.

Chapter

6 A TURBULENT TIME

❧⟨✕⟩❧

Launching the Black Star Line was just one of many major events in Marcus Garvey's life in 1919. In fact, his life nearly came to an end that year.

On October 14, Garvey was working in his Harlem offices as usual. As he sat at his desk, Garvey was confronted by George Tyler, a former employee. Tyler demanded money he said Garvey owed him. Before Garvey realized what was happening, Tyler pulled out a gun and fired several shots at Garvey. Though one bullet grazed his forehead and another lodged in his leg, Garvey escaped serious injury, thanks to the quick thinking of his secretary, Amy Ashwood. She tried to tackle Tyler, who quickly scrambled out of the office.

Tyler was caught the same day, but he died

Marcus Garvey was known for dressing in military or academic attire.

before his trial after falling from his jail cell window. Whether he committed suicide or died a more sinister death is still debated. Garvey claimed Tyler had been hired to assassinate him, but that was never proved. In any case, with Tyler now dead, police considered the matter closed.

The incident only served to make Garvey more popular. He now was a leader who had faced death and yet continued despite such danger to work to lead his people to better lives.

Thirty-two-year-old Marcus Garvey was photographed at his wedding to Amy Ashwood.

About two months after his brush with death, Garvey married his secretary, Amy Ashwood, in a lavish ceremony at Liberty Hall on Christmas Day. The two had met several years earlier at a debating society event in Kingston. Ashwood, who shared Garvey's vision for his people, had helped him found the UNIA in 1914. She visited him in New York City in 1918 and stayed on to become his chief assistant. However, the couple soon realized they were poorly suited to be husband and wife, and they separated

Garvey's first wife, Amy Ashwood Garvey, stood with members of the Friends of Ethiopia at a rally in London, England, in 1935.

three months after their marriage.

At the time, the United States was experiencing a time of unrest. Around 1920, the country was seized by labor strikes and increasing fear that communists and other radical political groups were gaining power. Public officials stepped up efforts to try to eliminate such groups.

Marcus Garvey was already a person of considerable interest to the U.S. government. The United States Bureau of Investigation, later known as the Federal Bureau of Investigation, or FBI, was watching Garvey. The government feared that his work was increasing tensions between whites and blacks—tensions that could lead to violence. As a result, he was seen as a potentially dangerous radical and was watched for any misstep. The Bureau of Investigation was looking for a reason to deport the man it saw as a troublemaker.

But Garvey had no intention of hiding. In August 1920, the UNIA held its first International Convention

Members of the ceremonial Garvey Milita stood at attention at a parade during a UNIA convention.

of the Negro Peoples of the World in New York. About 25,000 delegates from 25 countries attended the opening session at Madison Square Garden. The rest of the monthlong gathering was held at Harlem's Liberty Hall.

During the convention, the UNIA adopted a Declaration of the Rights of the Negro Peoples of the World and created a black, red, and green flag to represent its "nation." It also elected a provisional government. A Philadelphia minister, James Eason, was chosen as leader of the American Negroes, and Garvey was elected provisional president of Africa.

Because of Garvey's words and his new presidential title, leaders of the European colonies in Africa saw him as a threat. Because they did not trust him, Garvey would never be allowed into any African nation. ✆

7 AN AFRICAN SETTLEMENT

᭢᯽᭢

After the UNIA convention, Marcus Garvey pushed forward with plans to create a settlement in Africa for his followers. He tried to persuade the League of Nations to turn over to the UNIA the African colonies Germany had been forced to relinquish after World War I. Garvey was unsuccessful. But he was also interested in Liberia. As early as 1919, Garvey had announced his intent to move the UNIA's headquarters to Monrovia, the capital of Liberia.

Located on the west coast of Africa, Liberia was one of the few black-governed countries in Africa at the time. It was founded by freed American slaves sent to the continent by the American Colonization Society in the early 1800s. It became an independent nation in 1847. The capital was named after U.S.

British explorer, artist, and colonial administrator
Sir Harry Johnston painted a Liberian homestead.

Liberia has a unique history among African nations. Unlike other countries on the continent, it did not begin as a native state or as a European colony. Instead, it originated in 1822 with the establishment of a colony for free blacks from the United States. It was not the first such settlement, however. In 1787, the British resettled in Sierra Leone 400 free blacks who had fought with the British in the American Revolutionary War. There they founded the province of Freetown. Unlike Liberia, however, Sierra Leone was a British colony and remained under British rule until 1961.

President James Monroe, who was in office at the time the city was established.

In 1920, Garvey sent his trusted commissioner Elie Garcia to Monrovia to meet with Liberian officials and share the UNIA's plans. The plans included promoting emigration to Liberia, along with financial help for the impoverished nation. Garvey envisioned the establishment of schools, hospitals, and other facilities that would help the country.

In a report to Garvey, Garcia warned that the UNIA should downplay anything that suggested it might interfere with the government of Liberia. Garcia realized that government officials could see UNIA leaders as a threat to their power and control over their citizens. Garcia also noted that Liberian officials didn't want to anger the more powerful governments of the United States, Great Britain, and France. Since these nations saw Garvey and the UNIA as a threat to their interests in Africa, Liberian authorities needed to be careful in

their dealings with Garvey and his organization.

But Garvey didn't give up. In 1921, while he traveled to speaking engagements in Jamaica and Central America, he sent a UNIA delegation to Liberia to negotiate the formation of a UNIA community in the West African nation.

A steamer departed from Savannah, Georgia, taking 200 African-Americans to Liberia.

The 1921 UNIA Commission to Liberia was composed of G.O. Marke and Cyril A. Crichlow (seated, left to right) and Israel McLeod, A.N. Henry, F.L. Laurence, and Rupert Jemmott (standing).

At first the Liberian government seemed open to the UNIA's plan. In March, UNIA technicians arrived in Liberia to start setting up farms and buildings necessary to begin a settlement. At the time, the Black Star Line was still in operation and was expected to carry more supplies and immigrants to the settlement.

As the UNIA delegation continued to work out details with the Liberian government, Garvey was stranded in the West Indies. The U.S. State Department took advantage of the fact that Garvey had left the country and refused to allow him to come back on the ground that he was a dangerous radical. As Garvey tried to find a way back into the United States, Liberian President Charles King had a letter published in a black magazine called *The Crisis* assuring the world that Liberia would not allow itself to be used as a base for "aggression or conspiracy against other sovereign states." He assured other nations that their colonial interests in the area were safe.

In time, Garvey was able to get a visa, a permit that allowed him to re-enter the United States. He tried to assure President King that his fears of the UNIA were unfounded.

"We are not trying to use Liberia as a wedge to conquer all Africa," Garvey said. "But we believe Africa rightfully belongs to the Negro race."

Garvey continued for years to try to create a UNIA community in Liberia, but in the end, his efforts came to nothing.

8 "MARCUS GARVEY MUST GO"

Marcus Garvey's fierce love for his own race often put him in an unusual position. It sometimes led him to agree with some of America's most noted white racists. This, in turn, caused him to make enemies among members of his own race. Such was the case when Garvey decided to meet with the imperial wizard of the Ku Klux Klan (KKK), a white supremacist group.

On June 25, 1922, during a speaking tour, Garvey met for two hours in Atlanta, Georgia, with Edward Young Clarke, the leader of the KKK. During the meeting, which was held at Clarke's request, Garvey and Clarke each shared their beliefs. Clarke and his followers believed that the United States belonged to whites. He explained that the KKK wanted to keep

Marcus Garvey signed a 1924 photograph taken by James Van Der Zee, the UNIA's official photographer.

An 1874 political cartoon by Thomas Nast of "The Union As It Was: The Lost Cause—Worse Than Slavery"

the white race pure, meaning it did not believe in intermarriage between races. He also tried to convince Garvey that the KKK wasn't responsible for as many incidents of violence toward blacks as it was accused of. Garvey had written several editorials criticizing the KKK, whose members had threatened and even beaten some UNIA organizers in the South.

After the meeting, Garvey said he believed

that groups such as the KKK represented what white Americans really thought—that whites were superior to all other races. Garvey outraged even some of his own supporters by saying that the KKK and UNIA were alike in some ways. He said:

> *The Ku Klux Klan is the invisible government of the United States of America. The Ku Klux Klan expresses to a great extent the feeling of every real white American. The attitude of the Universal Negro Improvement Association is in a way similar to the Ku Klux Klan. Whilst the Ku Klux Klan desires to make America absolutely a white man's country, the Universal Negro Improvement Association wants to make Africa absolutely a black man's country.*

The Ku Klux Klan formed in Tennessee in May 1866 and quickly spread. Most of the group's leaders were former members of the Confederate army, which had been defeated by Union forces in the Civil War. Klansmen, draped in white sheets and covering their heads with masks and pointed hats, tortured and killed many black Americans, as well as those who sympathized with them. The KKK used fear to keep blacks from exercising their rights as citizens.

The meeting with Clarke served to cement in Garvey's mind the belief that blacks would never find equality in the United States. He believed even more firmly now that the UNIA should move forward with plans to create a strong government in Africa for the benefit of black people worldwide.

Meanwhile, groups such as the National Association for the Advancement of Colored People (NAACP) were taking a different path and working to overturn racist laws and push for equality. W.E.B. DuBois, one of the most influential black men of his era, headed the NAACP and believed the United States had a great deal to offer all people. He dreamed of the day when all races could live in the country in harmony while still remaining who they were. DuBois wrote:

W.E.B. DuBois
(1868–1963)

> He [the black man] simply wishes to make it possible for a man to be both a Negro and an American, without being cursed and spit upon by his fellows, without having the doors of Opportunity closed roughly in his face.

There were, of course, similarities between the NAACP and UNIA. Both supported anti-lynching laws and campaigned against Jim Crow laws, which included the withholding of voting rights from blacks

Blacks were forced to use a "colored" drinking fountain on the county courthouse lawn in Halifax, North Carolina.

and other forms of racial discrimination.

But that was where the similarities ended. Because he wanted blacks to rely only on themselves, Garvey rejected any help from whites. White people were not allowed to join the UNIA. They also were prohibited from owning shares in any of the businesses Garvey created. "We do not want their money," Garvey said. "This is a black man's movement."

The NAACP, on the other hand, welcomed help from anyone who supported the cause of equal rights for all, regardless of race.

Because each man believed so fiercely and exclusively in his approach to their mutual problem, DuBois and Garvey quickly turned hostile to one another. Both had public outlets for their venom. Garvey attacked DuBois and the NAACP in *The Negro World*. He said:

> The difference between the Universal Negro Improvement Association and the other movements of this country, and probably the world, is that the Universal Negro Improvement Association seeks independence of government, while the other organizations seek to make the Negro a secondary part of existing governments ... knowing that the Negro in America will never get his constitutional rights.

DuBois attacked Garvey in the NAACP's publication, *The Crisis*. He called Garvey "without a doubt, the most dangerous enemy of the Negro race in America."

Others in the United States found Garvey to be dangerous as well. Seeing Garvey as a troublesome radical, many high-ranking members of the NAACP held meetings as part of a "Marcus Garvey Must Go"

MARCUS GARVEY MUST GO!

Four of the Greatest Negro Meetings Ever Held in New York,

Sundays — August 6th, 13th, 20th and 27th

SHUFFLE INN MUSIC PARLORS

(Lafayette Building, Northeast Corner 131st Street and Seventh Avenue)

3 O'CLOCK SHARP

August 6th: **PROF. WILLIAM PICKENS,** Field Secretary of N. A. A. C. P.
Subject: WHAT TO DO WHEN NEGRO LEADERS LEAGUE WITH NEGRO LYNCHERS

August 13th: **A. PHILIP RANDOLPH,** Candidate for N. Y. Secretary of State
Subject: THE ONLY WAY TO REDEEM AFRICA

August 20th: **ROBERT W. BAGNALL,** Director of Branches for N. A. A. C. P.
Subject: THE MADNESS OF MARCUS GARVEY

August 27th: **CHANDLER OWEN,** Co-Editor of the MESSENGER.
Subject: A PRACTICAL PROGRAM FOR NEGROES EVERYWHERE

GARVEY'S STATEMENT AT NEW ORLEANS
"This is a white man's country. He found it, he conquered it, and we can't blame him if he wants to keep it. I am not vexed with the white man of the South for Jim-Crowing me, because I am black.
"I never built any street cars or railroads. The white man built them for his own convenience. And if I don't want to ride where he's willing to let me ride then I'd better walk."

All Invited — White and Colored, Men and Women — Native and Foreigner

Admission Free! Exactly One Thousand Seats

MEETINGS UNDER AUSPICES OF THE

FRIENDS OF NEGRO FREEDOM

campaign. They even wrote a letter to U.S. Attorney General Harry Daugherty asking that he get rid of Garvey. In time, they would get their wish. ✍

A flier repeated the NAACP's slogan, "Marcus Garvey Must Go!"

9 ON TRIAL AND IMPRISONED

For years, officials in the United States tried to use post office laws against Marcus Garvey. It was common for law enforcement officials to look for illegal use of the U.S. mail to trip up radical groups that spread their messages that way. Eventually the government was able to build a case against Garvey.

Garvey was arrested on January 12, 1922, on charges of mail fraud. The charges stated that Garvey had sent false and misleading Black Star Line advertisements through the mail. At his trial, which began in March 1923, Garvey chose to serve as his own lawyer. The move likely hurt his chance of winning the battle. Inexperienced in the courtroom, Garvey often argued with the judge and gave long-winded speeches that had no bearing on the case.

Marcus Garvey left court on February 6, 1925, after being sentenced to five years in the Atlanta Federal Penitentiary for mail fraud.

During the trial, which dragged on for more than a month, the prosecution showed that the Black Star Line had been terribly mismanaged. Garvey didn't pay attention to financial matters, which was a large part of the reason his business ventures failed. He also tended to reward loyal followers with jobs they weren't qualified for. He often put inexperienced or untrained people in important and powerful positions. Garvey was too stubborn to think they would fail or to admit that he may have been wrong for appointing them to these posts.

A Black Star Line stock certificate

The prosecution claimed that Garvey sent out

advertisements promising large profits to those who invested in the Black Star Line even after he realized the company was failing. The case rested on the shoulders of a stockholder named Benny Dancy, who allegedly bought stock in the company after receiving one of these advertisements in the mail.

As evidence, the prosecution produced an empty envelope bearing the Black Star Line stamp. The prosecution said that a letter promoting the company had been inside the envelope. However, while Dancy admitted he often received mail from the Black Star Line, he couldn't remember what had been in that particular envelope.

Nevertheless, Garvey was convicted of mail fraud. On June 21, 1923, the judge handed down the maximum sentence of five years in jail and a $1,000 fine. Garvey also was ordered to pay for the cost of the trial.

During the summer of 1923, Garvey was held at the Manhattan House of Detention, also known as "The Tombs." Though he was in

After his trial, Marcus Garvey warned of the dangers of a justice system that could convict a man based mainly on a flimsy piece of key evidence. He wrote: "To be convicted for using the mails to defraud on the evidence of a rubber stamped, empty envelope that could have been stamped and posted by any enemy or hired agent with the intent that prompted the prosecution, is a departure in our system that may lead to the incrimination and conviction of any man in our civilization who trespasses within the bounds or province where there is such a law."

The jail known as "The Tombs" opened in 1902.

jail, Garvey continued to make his voice heard. He used his time to write editorials for *The Negro World* that attacked his enemies and raised the spirits of his followers. He also wrote poetry. One poem, "Keep Cool," was later set to music and became an anthem for the UNIA.

Garvey's second wife, Amy Jacques Garvey, also helped him continue to spread his message. Once his private secretary, Amy Jacques had married Garvey July 27, 1922, a little more than a month after Garvey's divorce from his first wife was finalized. Amy Jacques Garvey understood her husband's devotion to the UNIA and supported him in his work. She even got a collection of his ideas published— the first volume of *The Philosophy and Opinions of Marcus Garvey*—while Garvey was in jail.

Amy Jacques Garvey (1895–1973)

Garvey was released pending his appeal in September 1923. For the next 15 months Garvey worked hard, and his followers continued to support him. With the financial support of UNIA members, Garvey launched the Black Cross Navigation and Trading Company. He also started the Negro Political Union (NPU). The NPU endorsed candidates for political office based only on their dealings with the black race and not on which political party they belonged to.

Garvey's months of freedom also were marked with disappointment. In 1924, Garvey's final large-scale effort to set up a community in Liberia was blocked by that country's government.

Another blow followed. The U.S. Supreme Court refused to hear Garvey's appeal of his mail fraud conviction. He was sent to the Atlanta Federal Penitentiary in February 1925. Garvey said that during his time in prison in Atlanta, he was given the hardest and dirtiest jobs, but he did them without complaint and to the best of his abilities. This drew the attention of the prison warden, J.W. Snooks. One day, Snooks called Garvey into his office. Realizing Garvey was doing his best even at the worst of jobs, Snooks rewarded Garvey by giving him better tasks.

A portion of Marcus Garvey's prison identification card

Meanwhile, Garvey's wife tried to secure a pardon for her husband from the U.S. government, but her efforts failed. However, she made sure Garvey's

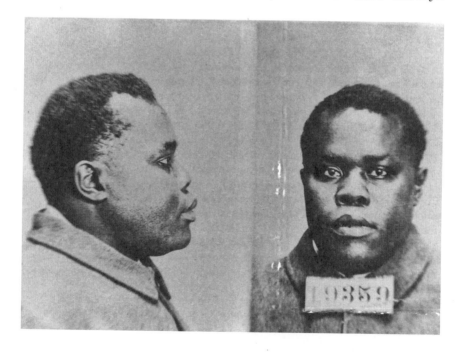

message would still be heard. In December 1925, she published the second volume of *The Philosophy and Opinions of Marcus Garvey*.

For a while, the UNIA continued to grow even though its leader remained in prison. So did public support for Garvey. About 150,000 people filled the sidewalks of Harlem during a march calling for Garvey's freedom. It was one of many demonstrations demanding Garvey's release.

The government had the option of freeing Garvey from prison and deporting him. At first, the attorney general, John Sargent, did not want to throw Garvey out of the country. As the attorney general, his role was to advise the president and serve as the U.S. government's top attorney. He felt Garvey and his message could better be controlled in prison. If Garvey were released from prison, he would be freer to spread his message, Sargent believed.

The attorney general wrote:

Marcus Garvey trusted his wife, Amy Jacques Garvey, to publish speeches, articles, and others materials he sent to her from prison in Atlanta, Georgia. He knew she would get them published word for word and not change the meaning of his writings. Amy felt deeply honored by his trust and wouldn't let him down, as she wrote in October 1925: "I have, at all times, endeavored to serve him who serves and suffers for his race; the compilation of this volume is but a slight effort in that direction. It is an honor and a pleasure to earn the confidence of one who has been, and is, so signally faithful to his sacred trust."

Marcus Garvey was impris-oned in the Atlanta Federal Penitentiary.

Garvey undoubtedly holds today an important and controlling influence over many thousands of the Negro Race in the United States, and while it may be that his further imprisonment will result in dissatisfaction to a greater or less extent, his release and deportation would by no means eliminate him as a menace. While a prisoner, his activities are subject to control, but with unrestricted freedom in another country to continue his propaganda, he might become even a greater menace to his own race and to society generally.

In time, however, the attorney general changed his mind. In a November 1927 message to President Calvin

Coolidge, Sargent said Garvey's sentence should be immediately commuted, meaning the president should grant Garvey's release. However, the attorney general counseled the president that Garvey should then be immediately deported.

Sargent's change of mind had nothing to do with a change in attitude toward Garvey. Instead the attorney general had realized that Garvey's continued imprisonment was seen by his followers as an act of oppression.

*U.S President
Calvin Coolidge
(1872–1933)*

The president followed Sargent's advice and commuted Garvey's sentence. Coolidge also ordered Garvey deported as an undesirable alien.

Garvey responded:

> *I had hoped that on my release from Atlanta I would have had the opportunity of returning to New York to straighten out the affairs of the Universal Negro Improvement Association, the Black Star Line and the Black Cross Navigation and Trading Company, but my enemies*

Uniformed attendees at a Garvey rally marched up Seventh Avenue in Harlem.

made sure of their game in not allowing me to return to New York. They had already swallowed up all the assets of the companies, which could be removed only by my presence in New York. So they skillfully influenced the Department of Labor and the Department of State to deport me to Jamaica. On the order of President Coolidge I was shunted to New Orleans, and from there to my homeland—Jamaica.

Before leaving the United States, Garvey said he was happy to suffer and even die for his cause.

He believed his work would continue even after his death. He told his followers:

> *Look for me in the whirlwind or the storm. Look for me all around you, for, with God's grace, I shall come and bring with me countless millions of black slaves who have died in America and the West Indies and the millions in Africa to aid you in the fight for Liberty, Freedom and Life.*

But the UNIA would never again be as strong as it once was. On December 3, 1927, about 5,000 followers braved the rain and sang "God Bless Our President" as the steamship carrying Garvey left New Orleans bound for Jamaica. Garvey would never come back to the United States. 🐚

RE TO THE WORLD
ST BE FREE

RIGHT EXCELLENT
MARCUS MOSIAH GARVEY
NATIONAL HERO
BORN AUGUST 17, 1887 – DIED JUNE 10, 1940.

JAMAICA NATIONAL TRUST COMMISSION

10 A LASTING LEGACY

Chapter

❧⟨✕⟩❧

News of Marcus Garvey's impending arrival was cause for celebration in his homeland. Crowds of people gathered at the dock and spilled into the streets of Kingston to wait for Garvey on December 10, 1927.

As the *Santa Marta* slowly moved toward the city's pier, Garvey stood on the deck. The crowd gave a thundering cheer when he came into view.

Members of the UNIA met their hero as he came ashore. He was ushered into a car that followed a parade in his honor through town to Kingston's Liberty Hall. Garvey's car moved slowly, giving him a chance to absorb the love of the crowd. Everyone wanted to see him or reach out and touch his shirtsleeve.

Garvey expected to speak to the crowd at Liberty

A statue of Marcus Garvey stands in his birthplace, St. Ann's Bay, Jamaica.

In 1919, Garvey had bought an auditorium at 120 W. 138th St. in Harlem, New York City, where he could host large meetings. He named the auditorium Liberty Hall. Over the years, the UNIA bought several buildings and called each of them Liberty Hall. In July 1923, the UNIA opened another Liberty Hall at 76 King St. in Kingston, Jamaica. Though the building in Jamaica fell into disrepair, the Friends of Liberty Hall, with the help of other organizations, launched a restoration project. The renovated building, now named "Liberty Hall: The Legacy of Marcus Garvey," reopened in October 2003.

Hall. However, when he got there, it was not clear that everyone who wanted to hear his words would fit in the building. Instead of going inside, Garvey stepped on the running board of his car and addressed the throng from there. In addition to thanking everyone for their support, he made them a promise: He told them he would spend the rest of his life trying to advance the cause of black people.

But Garvey's glory days were now just memories. No longer would he wield the power he had in the past. However, Garvey and the UNIA had blazed a path for other groups working for the rights of minorities to follow.

Garvey continued to try to reach out to others. In 1928, he traveled with his wife through Europe and Canada, spreading his message. He returned to Jamaica and tried to re-create the powerful base that he had once had in Harlem, but he wasn't successful. The groups attending his meetings grew smaller and smaller.

In 1929, Garvey became more directly involved in Jamaican politics. He created the People's Political Party (PPP) and ran for a seat on the legislative council. Still controversial, Garvey landed in jail on contempt charges after threatening to reform the court system if elected. His time in politics in Jamaica was marked by such events, but the PPP did find some success in electing

Although Garvey's movement was losing strength, UNIA parades were still well attended.

candidates to seats on the legislative council and the Kingston and St. Andrew Corporation council. Even Garvey was elected to serve a few years on the corporation council.

While in Jamaica, Garvey returned to some of his entrepreneurial activities. He ran a real estate and auctioneering business. He also returned to publishing, producing a magazine called *The Black Man*. According to an editorial in the first issue, the magazine was intended to be "the organ for reviving the great movement of the U.N.I.A. under new and honest leadership so that we may continue the battle for African redemption and for the development of the Negro race." The front cover of every issue featured a poem by Garvey, and regular inside features included Garvey's "letters to the Negro race."

On September 17, 1930, the Garveys welcomed their first child to the world, a son named Marcus Garvey Jr. In 1933, their family was complete with the addition of their son Julius.

Despite his growing family and shrinking audiences, Garvey sacrificed time with his wife and children to continue working to advance the causes of his race. He lectured in Canada and the Caribbean. One of his lifelong messages always remained the same: People needed to educate themselves in order to improve their lives. "Read! Read! Read! And never stop until you discover the knowledge of the

Universe," he told a crowd in St. Kitts in the British West Indies.

In 1935, Garvey moved to London, England, though Amy and the children remained in Jamaica. He continued to spread his beliefs through *The Black Man* and other publications. In 1938, Garvey created the School of African Philosophy. Through the school, Garvey offered classes and correspondence

Marcus Garvey returned to England in September 1936 after a convention in Canada.

courses to further spread his message and train UNIA organizers. Forty-two subjects were taught, and Garvey also offered personal instruction in grooming and leadership development. For all his efforts, however, only 11 students enrolled in the classes, and only eight signed up for the correspondence courses.

That year, Garvey's wife and sons traveled to London to join him. However, the boys were used to the warm climate of Jamaica, and they suffered from illnesses in chilly England. Marcus Jr. became

A 1938 aerial view of London, England

ill with rheumatic fever, and Julius was troubled by bronchitis. Garvey's wife and sons returned to Jamaica without him in September 1938. Garvey kept in touch with his family, writing them frequent letters, but he would never see them again.

On January 20, 1940, Garvey suffered a cerebral hemorrhage, or bleeding in his brain. It left him paralyzed on his right side and made it difficult for him to talk. He tried to conceal his condition when he appeared in public. He feared that showing any sign of weakness would give hope to the enemies of his cause.

On May 18, *The Chicago Defender* ran a story by a London reporter saying, inaccurately, that Garvey had died. Other stories followed, and soon Garvey's office was besieged by letters and visitors wanting to confirm the news. His secretary tried to keep him from finding out about the false reports, but Garvey eventually learned that he was widely believed to be dead. He was shocked and demanded that a statement be issued refuting the reports. But before he could finish dictating the statement, he suffered either a second cerebral hemorrhage or a heart attack. He died on June 10, 1940. He was 52 years old.

Garvey had wanted to be buried in Jamaica, but his wife didn't have the money to pay for his body to be transported to his homeland. Instead he was buried in London at St. Mary's Roman Catholic

Signature Lives

Cemetery. More than 20 years later, in November 1964, the Jamaican government brought his body home for its final burial. He was buried in the Marcus Garvey Memorial at National Heroes Park in Kingston. Garvey was declared Jamaica's first national hero, the highest honor in the country.

Although Marcus Garvey was criticized by many during his lifetime, the passage of time has led to a different view of Garvey and his achievements. Civil rights leader Martin Luther King Jr. told

Visitors pay their respects at Garvey's grave in Kingston, in Jamaica's National Heroes Park.

94

an assembly in 1965 honoring Garvey's memory:

> *Marcus Garvey was the first man of color in the history of the United States to lead and develop a mass movement. He was the first man, on a mass scale and level, to give millions of Negroes a sense of dignity and destiny, and make the Negro feel that he was somebody.*

In his lifetime, Marcus Garvey worked to end colonialism, calling Africa a country of the future that blacks would rise to govern as other men governed. But his most powerful message was one of racial pride and uplift. He made black people everywhere proud of their past and hopeful about their future—a future they would create for themselves. ⟡

The memory and vision of Marcus Garvey is honored in various ways around the world. People in Jamaica remember Garvey through their reggae music, many songs of which honor the memory of their national hero. Ghana, the first African country to gain independence from European colonial powers, named its national steamship line the Black Star Line.

GARVEY'S LIFE

1887

Born August 17 in
St. Ann's Bay, Jamaica

1901

Becomes a printer's
apprentice

1906

Moves to Kingston,
Jamaica, where he
works as a printer

1885   **1905**

1889

The Eiffel
Tower opens in
Paris, France

1903

Brothers Orville
and Wilbur Wright
successfully fly a
powered airplane

1909

Explorers
Robert E. Peary
and Matthew
Henson and
four Inuit reach
the North Pole;
they mark the
spot with an
American flag

WORLD EVENTS

1914
Creates the Universal Negro Improvement Association

1912
Moves to London, England, where he attends Birkbeck College

1916
Arrives in the United States to begin a year-long, cross-country speaking tour

1915

1916
German-born physicist Albert Einstein publishes his general theory of relativity

1914
Archduke Franz Ferdinand is assassinated, launching World War I (1914–1918)

1911
National Urban League is organized to help African-Americans secure equal employment

GARVEY'S LIFE

1919
Creates the Black
Star Line; marries
Amy Ashwood

1920
Launches the Negro
Factories Corporation

1922
Divorces Amy
Ashwood Garvey
and marries Amy
Jacques

1920

1920
American
women get the
right to vote

1919
The Treaty of
Versailles officially
ends World War I

1922
The tomb of
Tutankhamen is
discovered by
British archaeologist
Howard Carter

WORLD EVENTS

1925

Sent to prison in Atlanta, Georgia, after the U.S. Supreme Court refuses to review his case

1923

Fraud trial begins in New York

1927

Released from prison and deported from the United States; returns to Kingston, Jamaica

1925

1927

Charles Lindbergh makes the first solo nonstop transatlantic flight from New York to Paris

1923

Irish civil war ends and the rebels sign a peace treaty

1926

A.A. Milne publishes *Winnie the Pooh*

Garvey's Life

1930
Lectures in Canada and Europe; son Marcus Jr. born

1933
Son Julius born

1935
Moves to London, England

1930

1930
Clyde Tombaugh discovers Pluto; he was 24 years old

1933
Nazi leader Adolf Hitler is named chancellor of Germany

1936
African-American athlete Jesse Owens wins four gold medals at the Olympic Games in Berlin in the face of Nazi racial discrimination

World Events

1940

1940
Dies June 10 in London, England

1964
Body is returned to Jamaica and buried in National Heroes Park in Kingston

1939
German troops invade Poland; Britain and France declare war on Germany; World War II (1939–1945) begins

1945
The United States drops atomic bombs on Hiroshima and Nagasaki, Japan; World War II ends

1963
Martin Luther King Jr. delivers his "I Have a Dream" speech to more than 250,000 people attending the March on Washington

Life at a Glance

DATE OF BIRTH:	August 17, 1887
BIRTHPLACE:	St. Ann's Bay, Jamaica
FATHER:	Marcus Garvey (?–1920)
MOTHER:	Sarah Jane Richards Garvey (?–1908)
EDUCATION:	Church of England High School and 18 months at Birkbeck College (now part of London University in England)
FIRST SPOUSE:	Amy Ashwood Garvey (1897–1969)
DATE OF MARRIAGE:	December 25, 1919 (divorced June 15, 1922)
SECOND SPOUSE:	Amy Jacques Garvey (1895–1973)
DATE OF MARRIAGE:	July 27, 1922
CHILDREN:	Marcus Garvey Jr. (1930–) Julius Garvey (1933–)
DATE OF DEATH:	June 10, 1940
PLACE OF BURIAL:	National Heroes Park, Kingston, Jamaica

FURTHER READING

Caravantes, Peggy. *Marcus Garvey: Black Nationalist.* Greensboro, N.C.: Morgan Reynolds Pub., 2004.

Keller, Kristin Thoennes. *Booker T. Washington: Innovative Educator.* Minneapolis: Compass Point Books, 2007.

Lawler, Mary. *Marcus Garvey: Black Nationalist Leader.* Philadelphia: Chelsea House Publishers, 2005.

Mohamed, Paloma. *A Man Called Garvey: The Life and Times of the Great Leader Marcus Garvey.* Dover, Mass.: The Majority Press, 2003.

Schraff, Anne. *Marcus Garvey: Controversial Champion of Black Pride.* Berkeley Heights, N.J.: Enslow Publishers, Inc., 2004.

LOOK FOR MORE SIGNATURE LIVES
BOOKS ABOUT THIS ERA:

Benazir Bhutto: *Pakistani Prime Minister and Activist*

Fidel Castro: *Leader of Communist Cuba*

Madame Chiang Kai-shek: *Face of Modern China*

Winston Churchill: *British Soldier, Writer, Statesman*

Indira Gandhi: *Political Leader in India*

Jane Goodall: *Legendary Primatologist*

Adolf Hitler: *Dictator of Nazi Germany*

Queen Noor: *American-born Queen of Jordan*

Eva Perón: *First Lady of Argentina*

Joseph Stalin: *Dictator of the Soviet Union*

ON THE WEB

For more information on this topic,
use FactHound.

1. Go to *www.facthound.com*
2. Type in this book ID: 075653626X
3. Click on the *Fetch It* button.

FactHound will find the best
Web sites for you.

HISTORIC SITES
DuSable Museum of
African-American History
740 E. 56th Place
Chicago, IL 60637
773/947-0600
Exhibits on the historical experiences and
achievements of African-Americans

Marcus Mosiah Garvey Multimedia Museum
Liberty Hall
76 King St.
Kingston, Jamaica
876/948-8639/40
Interactive exhibits on Garvey's life
and message

alien
a citizen of one country who resides in
another country

correspondence courses
courses offered through the mail

discrimination
unfair treatment of a person or group, often
because of race or religion

entrepreneurial
having to do with setting up a business to
make money

lynching
killing by a mob without a trial, usually by hanging

oppression
an unjust or cruel exercise of authority or power

orator
someone who is skilled at public speaking

propaganda
information spread to try to influence the thinking
of people; often not completely true or fair

pulpit
elevated platform found in churches

racists
people who believe that one race is better
than another

supremacist
person who believes one group of people is better
than another

Chapter 1

Page 9, line 1: Robert A. Hill. *Marcus Garvey: Life and Lessons.* Berkeley: University of California Press, 1987, p. 9.

Page 10, line 11: Lawrence W. Levine. "Marcus Garvey's Moment: A Passionate and Perplexing Chapter in Black History." *The New Republic.* 29 Oct. 1984, p. 26.

Page 10, line 20: Marcus Garvey. *Selected Writings and Speeches of Marcus Garvey.* Mineola, N.Y.: Dover Publications, Inc., 2004, p. vi.

Page 10, line 24: E. David Cronon. *Black Moses: The Story of Marcus Garvey and the Universal Negro Improvement Association.* Madison: The University of Wisconsin Press, 1969, p. 66.

Page 13, line 24: Tony Martin. *Race First.* Dover, Mass.: The Majority Press, 1986, p. 41.

Page 15, line 4: Marcus Garvey. *The Philosophy and Opinions of Marcus Garvey: Volume 2.* Dover, Mass.: The Majority Press, 1986, p. 98.

Chapter 2

Page 18, line 4: Ibid., p. 124.

Page 21, line 5: Ibid., pp. 124–125.

Page 21, line 28: Ibid., p. 125.

Chapter 3

Page 32, line 2: Marcus Garvey. "Primary Sources: The Negro's Greatest Enemy." *American Experience: Marcus Garvey.* PBS.org 19 Nov. 2007. www.pbs.org/wgbh/amex/garvey/filmmore/ps_enemy.html

Chapter 4

Page 35, line 9: *The Philosophy and Opinions of Marcus Garvey: Volume 2,* p. 125.

Page 36, line 10: *Selected Writings and Speeches of Marcus Garvey,* p. 2.

Page 36, line 23: Ibid., p. v.

Page 36, line 28: *Black Moses: The Story of Marcus Garvey and the Universal Negro Improvement Association,* p. 18.

Page 37, line 1: Ibid., p. 17.

Chapter 5

Page 48, line 26: *Race First,* p. 155.

Page 50, line 1: Ibid.

Chapter 7

Page 65, line 8: Ibid., p. 125.

Page 65, line 16: Ibid.

Chapter 8

Page 69, line 9: *Selected Writings and Speeches of Marcus Garvey*, p. viii.

Page 70, line 18: W.E.B. DuBois. *The Souls of Black Folk.* New York: Barnes & Noble Classics, 2003, p. 9.

Page 71, line 7: *Race First*, p. 30.

Page 72, line 10: *The Philosophy and Opinions of Marcus Garvey: Volume 2*, p. 97.

Page 72, line 20: *Selected Writings and Speeches of Marcus Garvey*, p. vii.

Chapter 9

Page 77, sidebar: *The Philosophy and Opinions of Marcus Garvey: Volume 2*, p. 332.

Page 81, sidebar: Ibid., preface.

Page 82, line 2: *Race First*, p. 199.

Page 83, line 25: Herb Boyd. *Autobiography of a People.* New York: Doubleday, 2000, p. 246.

Page 85, line 5: Ibid., p. 244.

Chapter 10

Page 90, line 8: *Black Moses: The Story of Marcus Garvey and the Universal Negro Improvement Association*, p. 158.

Page 90, line 25: *Selected Writings and Speeches of Marcus Garvey*, p. iv.

Page 95, line 3: *Race First*, p. iii.

Boyd, Herb. *Autobiography of a People*. New York: Doubleday, 2000.

Cronon, E. David. *Black Moses: The Story of Marcus Garvey and the Universal Negro Improvement Association*. Madison: The University of Wisconsin Press, 1969.

DuBois, W.E.B. *The Souls of Black Folk*. New York: Barnes & Noble Classics, 2003.

Garvey, Marcus. *The Philosophy and Opinions of Marcus Garvey: Volume 2*. Dover, Mass.: The Majority Press, 1986.

Garvey, Marcus. "Primary Sources: The Negro's Greatest Enemy." *American Experience: Marcus Garvey*. PBS.org 19 Nov. 2007. www.pbs.org/wgbh/amex/garvey/filmmore/ps_enemy.html

Garvey, Marcus. *Selected Writings and Speeches of Marcus Garvey*. Mineola, N.Y.: Dover Publications, Inc., 2004.

Hill, Robert A. *Marcus Garvey: Life and Lessons*. Berkeley: University of California Press, 1987,

Levine, Lawrence W. "Marcus Garvey's Moment: A Passionate and Perplexing Chapter in Black History." *The New Republic*. 29 Oct. 1984.

Martin, Tony. *Race First*. Dover, Mass.: The Majority Press, 1986.

Morris, Leonard. *Questions and Answers: The Life of Marcus Mosiah Garvey*. Bloomington, Ind.: 1stBooks, 2002.

Africa, 12–13, 61. *See also specific nations.*
Africa for Africans, 10, 11–13, 36, 37, 51, 58, 65, 69, 79
American Colonization Society, 61
Ashwood Garvey, Amy (wife). *See* Garvey, Amy Ashwood.
Askia the Great (king of Songhay), 33
Atlanta Federal Penitentiary, 80

Belize, 40
black Americans, 38–39, 53, 61–62
Black Cross Navigation and Trading Company, 79, 83–84
black history, 10, 33
black homeland, 10, 11–13, 36, 37, 51, 58, 65, 69, 79
Black Man, The (magazine), 90
black pride, 10, 19, 37, 40–41
Black Star Line, 42–51, 53, 64, 75–77, 80, 83–84
Black Star Line Band, 9–10
Black Star Line (Ghana), 95
Britain. *See* Great Britain.
British Guiana, 40
British Honduras, 40
Burrowes, Alfred (godfather), 22–23

Chicago Defender, The (newspaper), 93
Church of England High School, 20
Civil War, 69
Clarke, Edward Young, 67–68, 69
Cockburn, Joshua, 45, 46
colonial governments, 12–13, 17, 18
communists, 57
Conahan, P.A., 20
Confederate army, 69
Coolidge, Calvin, 83, 84
Costa Rica, 28–30
Crisis, The (magazine), 65, 72
Cuba, 46, 47–48, 51

Dancy, Benny, 77
Daugherty, Harry, 73

Declaration of the Rights of the Negro Peoples of the World (UNIA), 10, 58
diseases, 31
Douglass, Frederick, 46
DuBois, W.E.B., 72, 80

Eason, James, 58
education, 10, 13, 20, 22, 33, 36, 90–92
England. *See* Great Britain.
Ethiopia, 13

farming, 17
Federal Bureau of Investigation (FBI), 58
flag, 11, 58
France, 62
Frederick Douglass (ship), 45. *See also Yarmouth* (ship)
Friends of Liberty Hall, 88

Garvey, Amy Ashwood (wife), 55, 56–57
Garvey, Amy Jacques (wife), 78–79, 80–81, 88, 90, 92–93
Garvey, Indiana (sister), 17
Garvey, Julius (son), 90, 91, 92–93
Garvey, Marcus, Jr. (son), 90, 91, 92–93
Garvey, Marcus (father), 17, 18–19, 21
Garvey, Marcus Mosiah
  in American politics, 79
  appearance of, 10
  attitude toward white people, 14–15
  birth of, 17
  on black control of Africa, 10, 13, 36, 37, 65, 69
  books by, 79, 81
  burial of, 93–94
  as businessman, 44–45, 46, 53, 76, 79
  childhood of, 17, 20–21
  death of, 93
  deportation of, 81–85, 87

Brenda Haugen started in the newspaper business and had a career as an award-winning journalist before finding her niche as an author. Since then, she has written and edited many books, most of them for children. A graduate of the University of North Dakota in Grand Forks, Brenda lives in North Dakota with her family.

Image Credits